In the Deep

Mary Chiara

Jasper House

In the Deep

Contents

For the chronic illness community, and anyone who has ever
felt unheard.

Foreword

My previous collection of poetry, *Light Through the Leaves*, shared the highs, lows, and in-betweens one person can experience in just a brief time of their life. The overarching message throughout the book is that there is always light that will shine through the darkness, and that you are never alone in what you endure.

My new collection of poetry, titled *In the Deep*, takes on a more serious tone. These poems pertain to a more trying time in my life and writing them has been an outlet for release and healing. The light still shines through, but not without first acknowledging the darkness.

I thank you for joining me on this journey as we learn, struggle, and prevail together in the deep.

Premature Peace

And now,
Everything I'd gained
I've lost
On a summer's evening
When the air is thick
In the humid bath
Of breaking light
When the piano music
Heavy with melodic thunder
Circles the walls
And tries to pull me under
As the curtain is drawn
And the rings all rattle
In this empty chamber
Where I dwell in wonder
While the words of the day
Calm my mind with lies
And the heat inhales me
As I close my eyes

Dream Away

The waterfall washed away the log
Pushed it right over the cliff like a twig
And it sank lower and lower
Suspended in free fall
Waiting for the inevitable crash

I Dream at Dawn

Late nights swirl into hazy dim mornings
Does it really make a difference
I'm always tired behind my eyes

Eyes fall closed on a two-lane road
I'm not really sure how I got there
I remember not letting myself drive

The quiet makes my ears ring
The dark brings out the shadows
Lying still reminds me of my pain

The sheets are like sandpaper on my skin
Is there any air left in this room
I could never sit still

Finally morning comes again
My brain and body start to settle
The alarm clock tells me it is safe to sleep

The Dam

What once felt blocked
Now feels cracked
On the way to free-flowing

I Wish You Could See It from My Point of View

The little comments, eye rolls, and sighs
Don't go unnoticed
Always walking the line
Between what's acceptable and what makes you uncomfortable
It's all in the name of pride
But who's pride gets to live untarnished

Twisted Tea

The loneliness stings like too-hot tea on the tongue
Only tepid and tasteless if times are so fun
Torture and torment tied in lies that are spun
Making twisted webs to tell together I have none

Creative Mess

When I think about the inside of my brain

I see an art room
Creations in every corner
But none really go together
Some are titled and proudly displayed
Others scribbles and sketches of passing ideas
A forgotten lump of clay drying up on the windowsill
A paint brush abandoned half washed in the sink
Piles of paper, stacks of canvas, buckets of paint

Everything one could need to make anything they dream,
But too much of a mess to find what they need to create

Destiny

I don't know why God chose me
I guess because I asked Him to
Sometimes I forget that I knew
What I was getting into

Unraveling

Why must change be so hard to accept
Unless it is our own?
Life is like a ball of yarn
That slowly becomes unraveled
A little more each year
We grasp so tightly to the skein
Ignoring pleas to be knit into a showpiece
There is so much to do with what we have
Yet we tie knots in each other's creations
As if we are creators
Why do you tie so many knots in my string
When we could be tying ours together?
Blind to the realization our yarn is the same
So accept me as I am with each new day
And I'll accept your change

You're Right - It's All an Act

I have to pretend I'm not in pain because you feel you have more of a right to be

I have to pretend I'm having fun because that is all you want from me

I have to pretend I'm not exhausted because you don't see how I have a reason to be

I have to pretend to not notice your eye rolls and under-the-breath comments because you will never believe me

I have to pretend I can relate to what you say because if I don't what will our friendship be

I have to pretend I don't have certain issues because if you know I do you won't treat me

I have to pretend everything is perfect because if I don't what kind of professional would I be

I have to pretend it isn't hard to keep up because that is how you know me

I have to pretend I am doing better because that is all you choose to see

Turn My Page, Please

Your favorite book you will read
A hundred times
The same words, the same story
Yet you cling to every word
How do I become
A favorite story?

Secrets We Keep

Say we don't want it
Know it may never be ours
Protecting our hearts

In the Red

I wish that love was free
But it always comes at a price
The cost of opportunity

Love is Patient

Last night you held me
For far longer than I hoped
Loved me for my needs

Food for Thought

No room to complain, not really
When food is always in the cupboard
Seems wrong to be upset
To not be able to eat any of it
Without feeling sick

At least it is there
It might be unhealthy for my body
It might cause great distress
But it sits there on a shelf undisturbed

It must serve some good
Than to just tease and torture
It is there but it is not for me
But it is there
So, there will be no complaint today.

Just One More Time

I don't know what to say
Other than that I would do anything
To go back

I don't care how far back
Ten years before, two months before, the day before
Just take me back

The comforts you don't even know
You shouldn't take for granted until they're gone
If I could just have one back

No Spoons in the Drawer

There's no spoons in the drawer today

Someone must have forgotten to run the dishwasher

Minus one spoon for you to start the day

Stand up, make the bed

A spoon falls to the floor

Make breakfast, get dressed

One spoon more

Go to work, go to school, go where you need to go

Five spoons clatter as they trail behind you on the ground

The day drags on and you start to slow

You search for extras but no hidden spoons are found

Make dinner, take a shower

Three spoons fall down

It takes everything in your power

To not let yourself drown

In the fatigue, in the pain

One spoon over for the day

Tomorrow's loss is today's gain

You Act Like I Am

Can you please acknowledge that what I'm feeling is real?

Routine exam, routine questions, routine responses

Answers you don't know and refuse to find form a heavy cloud
of tension between us

Zip! There you go fleeing the room as fast as you can

Your failure feels like my own

Words for the Voice in My Head

Oh little voice in my head
We both wish each other were dead
You think you're so cool
But you're just a fool
Who fears what's solidly said

But it isn't just you
Oh how weak I am too
I wish you would leave me alone
To hear no more of your drone
Can't wait for the day that we're through

The Vase

Growth is hollow
Like a vase once filled with air
The flowers bloom then wilt
The water must be replaced
An endless cycle of beauty and death

Self-Love

She loved herself, so she ate ice cream
She loved herself, so she wore a short skirt
She loved herself, so she bought Starbucks
She loved herself, so she danced for TikTok

She loved herself, so she ate organic foods
She loved herself, so she went outside
She loved herself, so she did Pilates
She loved herself, so she went down and up with the sun

She loved herself, so she said just that and prayed it's all
she'd need

The Wooden Boat

It's a little wooden boat with two oars and just one hole

Making its way blissfully down the stream

Dock up ahead, waiting patiently

Except the dock seems to not be getting any closer?

Please, please, that can't be right!

Row, row! Row the boat - faster, faster!

Exit the boat! What once sank slow now sinks rapidly

Swim for the dock! What do you mean you don't know how?

Swim, girl! Swim, boy! You - swim!

Escape before you drown! You must figure out how!

Death awaits those who have no lifeguard, who were given no swimming lessons

The Locket

Clasped tightly in the hands of the Giver
A gift for only one Receiver
All the secrets of the World are under one lock
The Giver must fight off the flock
While time ticks down on the ever-beating clock

A War erupts in the evening
Breaking and beating and Thieving
The Giver stands strong, the Giver stands proud
For if they run from the Crowd
The Receiver will never be found

The battle is captured by Night
'Til only Two are left in the light
A secret Exchange
Of no small Change
Amidst the Firing range

The Receiver wears the prize
Then Realizes what it implies
There's no Escape
They must wear the Cape
All the days of their life

Figure Eights

Footsteps in the snow
Making figure eights wherever I go
Future hopelessly unknown

An answer to a prayer
With a question hanging in the air
Will it remain unimpaired

All roads will take you there
No single path is truly fair
But not all ways can be compared

Tightrope

The thin cord bounces lightly under my feet
I stand halfway across, rising and falling with the motion
Brought back to childhood moments of trampoline playing
Tempted to give in to the fun and jump my heart out
But the risk of falling is far too great

Much Too Young

Her middle name is Too Young
They read it off her chart as they check her in
And again when they take their notes
Once more when they say it's time to go

She hates her name but others must think it is pretty
Because they say it each time they see her
Usually with a disbelieving laugh that she doesn't understand
She says their name and laughs back

How troubling it must be
To be much Too Old
To have lived so long so peacefully
That the first storms within take such a great toll

But she is named for her hurricane
She is greeted with her full name wherever she goes
Anyone who shares her name should expect the same
Shouldn't anyone who must have named themselves?

Diagnosis

What do you have?
It's as natural an inquiry as any
Yet the words tangle up in my throat
Like my brush catching on a knot in my hair
When I try to respond casually

What do I have, I ask myself often
Who do I trust when the data is a scatter plot
How do I connect the dots?
And why am I the one to connect the dots?
They ask my medical background

My medical background? Let's count
The years of illness
And tests
And doctors
And judgements
Of is this symptom a trip to the ER or just another night

Medical training? Is that a joke?
Because they have written my words verbatim
And signed their name beneath them
Trusted with a history, tests, diagnoses, and treatments
But never with the suggestion to look deeper

How can I tell you what I have
When Medical Background disagrees with
Medical Background
And I am spun around and around
Come back in six months
For what? The answer to everyone's question?

Or to remind me that I can't move forward without
More expensive treatment, why don't you start a GoFundMe,
Ask your friends and your family, and don't forget to pay
The five hundred dollars on the way out

The End

At some point I will be standing on a mountain
and a dove will land next to me
And I will know that we had been doing this
together the entire time

In the Deep - A Cry for Advocacy

In the deep I fall
It is easy to be sucked in
To a swirling, spinning sea

When it first pulls me under
I feel alone in the darkness
Floating in the heavy pressure

A little deeper though, and I feel
The brush of a limb against me
My eyes open and I see the bodies

At first there is relief in their presence
Until I realize they are drowning too
I would rather be alone than be joined in suffering

I wonder why it's so dark here
Shouldn't there be a searchlight?
Why is no one trying to save this sinking, dying crowd

I hear laughter on the surface
As oblivious people swim right by
The crowd splashes and flails to try to grab their attention

But their laughter only grows louder
And it is then that I realize
We are completely invisible